Contents

Abstract

Since the advent of neo-liberalism in Mexico nearly 30 years ago, the country has seen sustained economic growth, particularly in the service and industrial export sectors. There is potential for this growth to continue and for Mexico to become one of the ten largest economies on the globe, but in order for this to happen there will need to be reliable and widespread access to energy. While natural gas is rapidly becoming the predominant energy source in Mexico, the future of the natural gas industry there is in doubt. This paper assesses the status of Mexico's natural gas industry, particularly with respect to transportation and distribution infrastructure, against current and projected demand. The role and impact of Mexico's state-owned petrochemical company, both past and present, are examined, as well as the influence of government policies and politics. The paper arrives at conclusions regarding the adequacy of Mexico's existing natural gas infrastructure and ends with recommendations as to how leaders in government and industry can bring about needed changes to both preserve and enhance the natural gas industry and the nation's overall economy.

Introduction

The advent of neo-liberalism under President Miguel de la Madrid (1982-1988) marked the beginning of Mexico's transition to a market-based economy after decades of corporatism and import-substitution-industrialism (ISI) had failed to achieve stable industrial growth and instead had taken the country to the brink of economic collapse.[1] While not without hardship, the neo-liberal movement was successful at sparking sustained growth in the service and industrial export sectors, and the past three decades have seen Mexico's economy grow to rank as the world's 11th largest.[2] However, Mexico's burgeoning economy now faces an uncertain future as its leaders in government and industry come to grips with the unavoidable truth that sustained economic growth requires reliable and affordable access to energy. While many areas of Mexico's economy have been successfully privatized, the petrochemical industry remains largely a government monopoly. Seventy years of nationalized control of this industry have resulted in diminishing production levels, as well as inadequate and aging transportation and distribution infrastructure. Natural gas, the energy source of choice for much of Mexico's current and projected industrial growth, is an area of particular concern as Mexico's natural gas production, transportation, and distribution infrastructure is inadequate to meet the needs of its growing economy. The government of Mexico must take concerted and decisive action to create and implement new and revised policies governing natural gas transportation and distribution in order to achieve the infrastructure improvements and expansions needed to support continued economic growth. To support this position, the author will explore current conditions as well as past, present and planned development of Mexico's natural gas industry, and the role of politics and national policy.

A Brief History of Mexico's Petrochemical Industry

Understanding the history of Mexico's nationalized petrochemical industry is central to understanding the current challenges the country faces with its natural gas infrastructure. Oil was first discovered in Mexico at the turn of the last century. Mexican law at the time gave surface owners subsurface mineral rights as well. A 1917 amendment to Article 27 of the Mexican Constitution made all subsurface minerals the property of the state, but was then further amended to honor pre-existing agreements with private owners. Under this framework the Mexican oil industry was dominated by private "Big Oil" companies from the United States and Britain, and the nation grew to become the second largest oil producer in the world.[3] A series of disputes between the Mexican government and private oil companies, including the refusal of these companies to honor a Mexican court ruling regarding wages and compensation for Mexican workers, led President Lezaro Cardenas (1934-1940) to expropriate Mexico's oil reserves (along with all other sub-surface mineral rights) in 1938.[4]

One development born out of President Cardenas' move to nationalize these oil reserves was a fierce sense of patriotism and pride amongst the population. In his address to the Mexican population announcing the expropriation, President Cardenas coined the phrase, "El petroleo es nuestro" (The oil is ours), and these words have been used by Mexican presidents and politicians to appeal to national pride ever since.[5] Public support for nationalizing oil was overwhelming at the time and is still celebrated as a Mexican national holiday, Oil Expropriation Day, on March 18th of every year.[6] This strong national pride in the country's natural resources, and corresponding fear that these resources might be unfairly exploited by private companies, has contributed to politics behind existing laws and policies that are hampering growth and development in Mexico's petrochemical industry.

2

Petroleos Mexicanos (PEMEX) is the state-owned company created in 1938 to run the national oil and natural gas monopoly. In the decades that followed, PEMEX often utilized private companies and contractors in order to maximize oil and gas production, and development of new reserves. These private companies and contractors were often rewarded via incentivized contracts tied to production levels. In 1958 however, in a move influenced by the "El petroleo es nuestro" mindset, Mexican law was further amended to ban in-kind payments and other incentives related to production levels.[7] This and other adverse regulatory policies in Mexico have severely limited PEMEX's ability to attract private investment to help address its infrastructure needs.

Stay the Course?

Most experts agree that Mexico's natural gas infrastructure is lacking, but there is disagreement on how to address the problem. A major point of contention is the debate on whether or not to allow (or expand) private investment in the natural gas industry, particularly in upstream areas relating to production. Those in favor of retaining state control point to other options for addressing the shortfalls in natural gas production, transportation, and distribution.

One argument against privatization is that, despite PEMEX's less than illustrious track record, the company possesses the leadership, experience, and resources to deal with the infrastructure problems itself. The Party of the Democratic Revolution (PRD), the democratic socialist party in Mexico, is one such group that has opposed recent proposals by President Felipe Calderon's (2006-present) to expand privatization of PEMEX and its subsidiaries. The PRD has proposed an alternate plan, developed by founding PRD member and adviser to the National Commission for Energy Conservation, Dr. Claudia Sheinbaum Pardo:

> PRD's proposed adjustments to PEMEX would reintegrate it as one whole functioning body rather than its present division into independent sectors. This move towards integration would unify all parts of PEMEX, from exploration of oil fields to commercialization of the final product. An assimilated industry would facilitate and lower expenses in the production/value chain, which is currently costing the company more than $20 billion annually.[8]

While Dr. Pardo's proposal may seem reasonable, history indicates that the plan is overly optimistic in assuming that PEMEX has the ability to function in a coherent and efficient manner. During much of the past seven decades since its creation, PEMEX enjoyed the benefit (as described by Pardo) of being, "one whole functioning body," yet during its time at the helm PEMEX has essentially driven Mexico's natural gas industry onto the rocks. In fact, PEMEX has been described as resembling, "a poorly run government ministry,"[9] and the condition of the country's natural gas infrastructure reflects this depiction.

Another argument offered by proponents of maintaining the status quo of nationalized oil and gas is that, because Mexico is still a net oil exporter, a portion of these oil exports could be used domestically to offset shortfalls in natural gas. This idea has numerous flaws, not least of which is that PEMEX's oil transportation and distribution infrastructure is in as bad or worse shape than the natural gas infrastructure.[10] Another significant factor impacting any decision regarding oil substitution is the increased level of pollution generated by oil burning facilities as opposed to modern natural gas fired co-generation plants. In keeping with worldwide agreements such as the Kyoto treaty, Mexico has enacted policies to encourage the use of natural gas and the conversion of existing oil-burning facilities to natural gas, and turning to oil substitution would be a step backwards.[11]

Problems from well-head to burner head

Mexico's natural gas infrastructure suffers in both quantity and quality across the spectrum, from the source to the end user. Analysis and discussion of existing and projected shortfalls in infrastructure are facilitated by first looking at the current gas transport system in Mexico. Figure 1 shows the layout of natural gas transport pipelines and facilities in Mexico. Some key of the key infrastructure shown include: Cuidad Juarez in the Northwest (the main import point for gas from the United States), Reynosa-Burgos in the Northeast (Mexico's primary source of gas not associated with oil, known as dry gas, representing roughly 17% of domestic production), Cuidad Pemex in the South (the country's primary source of gas associated with oil, known as wet gas, representing 80% of domestic production), and Los Ramones, which is the junction of these three principal sources of gas supply.[12] With the existing network, the lion's share of Mexico's natural gas production (near Cuidad Pemex in the South) is connected with its region of greatest demand in the North through a single pipeline. This creates a chokepoint for gas flow and presents a serious vulnerability and lack of redundancy.

In the past decade liquified natural gas (LNG) has become another key source of imported natural gas in Mexico, particularly for the state run electrical power company, Compania Federal de Electricidad (CFE). LNG terminals are in operation at Altimira, Costa Azul and Manzanillo, and a forth terminal is under construction in Sonora (see figure 1). Additional LNG terminals are planned near existing facilities in Costa Azul and Manzanillo, but they will provide gas directly to electrical power plants and not be tied into the national pipeline network. Only the facility at Sonora, when completed, will inject gas into PEMEX's pipeline network for domestic transportation and distribution.[13]

Mexico's natural gas infrastructure will be examined in three segments: upstream infrastructure for production or importation of gas, mid-stream pipelines and facilities for transportation and storage of gas, and downstream networks for distribution of gas. A fourth area of discussion will be physical security, an overarching area of concern for all segments of Mexico's natural gas infrastructure.

Sitting on the solution?

The challenges facing Mexico's natural gas infrastructure begin upstream with production. Roughly 17% of Mexico's nationwide demand for natural gas had to be fed with imports in 2010. With growth in demand outpacing production, imports are projected to account for 21% or more of total demand by 2015.[15] The United States and Japan are proof that supplying national energy demand solely with domestic production is not a pre-requisite for strong economic growth, but Mexico has real potential to meet and exceed its energy demands solely from domestic supply, with the accompanying increase in jobs and revenue. Yet, despite its vast proven and unproven reserves, Mexico has become a net importer of natural gas. Many factors have contributed to PEMEX's inability to meet domestic demand for natural gas, but there are two principal causes: lack of emphasis on exploration and development of new production, and lack of critical infrastructure in areas currently in production.

While not directly related to the production, transportation, and distribution of natural gas, it is worth noting the impact resulting from PEMEX's lack of exploration and development of oil and gas reserves. Given the extent of existing proven reserves in Mexico and adjacent oil fields in the United States, it is widely believed that there are significant undiscovered reserves of oil and gas lying under Mexico's lands and oceans, yet PEMEX has explored only 20% of the potential oil and gas producing regions.[16] Despite this lack of overall exploration, PEMEX has proven reserves of oil and associated gas in the Gulf of Mexico, but lacks the in-house ability to exploit them.[17]

Similarly, PEMEX has vast proven reserves of non-associated gas near Burgos along the Mexican-U.S. border in the North, but lacks the organic capability to effectively tap into these shale reserves. "Burgos' reserves represent 57.1 percent of total natural gas reserves but contribute only 17.3 percent to total natural gas production."[18] It is telling that these shortfalls in production were predicted years ago but recommendations on how to avoid them were not acted upon. A study conducted nearly a decade ago projected the rise in domestic natural gas demand in Mexico by 2010 and outlined $18 billion in recommended investments towards increased exploration and production in order to satisfy this growing demand.[19] The study's projections regarding growth in natural gas demand have proven to be quite accurate, but its recommendations were ignored and imports of natural gas in the past decade have grown significantly as demand has outpaced production.

Up in smoke

Nearly as troubling as PEMEX's inability to identify and exploit its proven and unproven reserves of natural gas is its failure to effectively utilize all of the natural gas currently being brought up as associated wet gas in oil production. In crude oil production, when oil is pumped out of the ground or seabed, natural gas trapped in the oil is released. There are three typical options for what to do with this associated gas. One is to capture and process the gas for transportation, distribution and sale. A second option is to re-inject the gas back into the wells, where it serves as "lift gas" making the oil easier to pump up out of the well. The third option is to simply burn off or vent the escaping gases in a process known as gas flaring. In order of difficulty and complexity from an infrastructure perspective, gas flaring is the easiest option and processing the gas for local use or commercial distribution is the most difficult.[20]

Due to a lack of adequate infrastructure at many of its oil production facilities, PEMEX flares off a significant amount natural gas annually. In 2009, PEMEX flared off more than $3 billion worth of natural gas, equivalent to nearly a quarter of the country's natural gas imports that year.[21] Not only does this practice rob the country of potential revenue, it also gives the nation a black eye environmentally due to the carbon emissions associated with gas flaring. The gas flaring practices of PEMEX reflect the short-sighted approach taken by the company and the Mexican government with respect to developing its natural gas infrastructure. Investing in the necessary infrastructure to capture, process, and transport the gas currently being flared would cost several billion dollars up front, but would return tens or hundreds of billions of dollars in the long run. Unfortunately, the "pay me now" mindset of the Mexican government has prevented this and other seemingly obvious capital improvements from occurring.

Another area for improvement lies with PEMEX's significant use of natural gas as lift-gas. While not as wasteful as gas flaring and less polluting, use of natural gas as lift-gas is far from optimal. With the right processing infrastructure, nitrogen and other gases or fluids like water or steam can be used to create the "artificial lift" needed to enhance oil production.[22] Another option is to process the associated gas from oil production, removing carbon dioxide (CO_2) for use as lift gas, and preserving the natural gas for distribution. This method not only increases the effective production rate of natural gas, it reduces green-house emissions by pumping the chief offender (CO_2) back into the wells.[23] However, due to a lack of infrastructure and development, PEMEX has failed to capitalize on these options. PEMEX not only holds the monopoly on natural gas production in Mexico, it is also its own biggest customer, consuming over 40% of annual natural gas production to support its oil industry operations.[24] If all or most of the natural gas currently consumed for lift gas were able to be preserved for distribution using the alternative methods of artificial-lift described above, it could potentially close the existing gaps between domestic production and demand, and likely make Mexico a net exporter of natural gas.

Mexico's gas pipelines, old and inadequate

Where the production segment of Mexico's natural gas industry suffers primarily from simple lack of infrastructure and development, its mid-stream pipeline and storage networks not only lack coverage and capacity, but also face a looming crisis of age and obsolescence. PEMEX's existing oil and gas network has been described as including, "A network of 36,738 kilometers of deteriorating pipelines drape[d] across the Mexican landscape," and recent estimates put the price of repairing known deficiencies at $9 billion or more.[25] In addition to repairs, the existing pipeline networks require numerous upgrades in storage and processing capability. While modern pipelines utilize distributed storage and incremental compression facilities to maintain pressure and volume, Mexico's antiquated system lacks these features. PEMEX has traditionally relied on a technique known as line pack in lieu of dedicated storage facilities. "Line Pack [is] [t]he ability of a natural gas pipeline to effectively "store" small quantities of gas on a short-term basis by increasing the operating pressure of the pipe."[26] Prior to the large growth in domestic natural gas demand over the past decade, line pack offered adequate "in-pipe" storage for PEMEX to account for fluctuations in daily demand, but this is no longer feasible especially given the safety concerns with increasing pressures in the aging pipeline network.[27]

The problems associated with PEMEX's lack of distributed gas storage facilities are exacerbated by an inadequate number of compression stations and further complicated by geography. Roughly 80% of PEMEX's domestic production of natural gas is generated in the South and enters its pipeline network at Cuidad Pemex. Meanwhile, the region of fastest growing demand lies in the North, fed by the single pipeline discussed earlier. The combined factors of distance, a single pipeline chokepoint, lack of compression station capacity, and growing demand in Northern Mexico highlight the shortcomings of PEMEX's existing natural gas infrastructure.

> The national pipeline system will have to be reinforced with incremental compression, pipeline replacement, looping, and new pipelines in order to handle a total flow of at least 8 bcfd in 2010. Storage will be needed as line pack management in the national pipeline system-used now in lieu of storage becomes exhausted.[28]

These recommended improvements were contained in the same industry study mentioned previously when discussing domestic gas production. Similar to the study's recommendations on how to increase production, its recommendations to improve and modernize PEMEX's existing pipeline networks have gone largely unheeded. There have been some pipeline improvements, such as the Supervisory Control And Data Acquisition (SCADA) system installed a decade ago.[29] However, the SCADA system, while greatly enhancing PEMEX's remote monitoring and control abilities, is little more than a band-aid on the larger problem of overall obsolescence within its existing pipelines.

In addition to the many improvements and modernizations needed to sustain its existing pipeline network, PEMEX also needs to expand its network to accommodate and stimulate future economic growth in the country. With natural gas the cheapest and cleanest fossil fuel, followed by its cousin liquid petroleum gas (LPG), it is no surprise that demand is so strong. The electrical power generation industry is the fastest growing consumer of natural gas in Mexico, with annual growth of nearly 15% in recent years, and along with other markets such as the manufacturing industries, and residential, commercial and municipal customers, is expected to drive up total demand for natural gas in Mexico by 10% a year for the remainder of this decade.[30]

Many potential customers are not waiting around while PEMEX wrestles with the challenges of inadequate production and pipeline infrastructure. The growing electrical generation industry is a prime example. A combination of growing electrical demand in the United States and reduced regulatory restrictions in Mexico have led to rapid growth in the electrical production industry. Unlike with its petrochemical industry, Mexico has allowed significant private investment in electrical power production. The number of independent power producers (IPP) in Mexico is growing rapidly and many are utilizing liquid natural gas (LNG) to power their facilities due to the lack of coverage by PEMEX. This is particularly true in the Northwest and along Mexico's pacific coast. These LNG terminals, described previously, are not connected to PEMEX's national pipeline grid and instead feed directly to IPP co-generation power plants. The private companies associated with the IPP ventures plan to export any future excess capacity North across the border into the United States.[31]

These existing LNG terminals and associated pipelines, licensed and approved by Mexico's energy ministry, Comisión Reguladora de Energía (CRE), have helped to make up for shortfalls in PEMEX's domestic production, transportation and distribution and allow for continued growth in the power industry. However, they are not the best long term solution. Unlike domestic supply from PEMEX's own reserves, the natural gas supplied through LNG terminals is subject to worldwide supply and demand and associated market volatility, with the accompanying risk of rising prices and lack of availability. Given the potential of Mexico's known reserves, the better long term solution is to expand PEMEX's pipeline network to provide better access to the industries and customers driving projected future demand. Just as there have been expert recommendations regarding infrastructure repair and modernization, so too are there assessments on the scope of new natural gas transportation and distribution infrastructure required. In his article, Raul Monteforte outlines the recommended expansion of natural gas infrastructure in Mexico, including extensive new pipeline networks, additional cross-border pipelines, more storage capacity, and LNG terminals tied into the PEMEX network and supplied by PEMEX gas from off-shore wells.[32] The magnitude of these recommended expansions, both in physical scope and projected cost, is daunting especially given the historical lack of funds available to PEMEX for capital reinvestment. As will be discussed further, the most viable option is to fund the majority of these improvements through private investment.

Gas Distribution... getting it to the customer

The third segment of Mexico's natural gas infrastructure, local distribution, also faces challenges. Even if the natural gas production and transportation networks were adequate, there still needs to be a system to distribute the gas to the many thousands of existing and potential customers. For high volume users such as power and manufacturing companies the economies of scale simplify the situation, allowing for dedicated connections directly to PEMEX's pipeline or proprietary pipelines from LNG terminals. For medium, small and micro businesses, as well as municipalities and residential customers, gaining access to natural gas supply is more complicated. Legal changes made in 1995 opened up downstream distribution of natural gas to private investment, but challenges remain. Political and regulatory roadblocks are hampering the creation and expansion of end user distribution networks and preventing the associated economic growth they would create.[33] Resolving this problem will require constitutional and regulatory changes to allow contract terms more enticing and less risky to private investors. Some areas, such as Mexico City, have seen improvements in access to natural gas and LPG in recent years, but the less than favorable contract terms currently available under Mexican law are causing potential investors to shy away.[34] There are numerous success stories where countries such as Argentina, Columbia and Brazil have made the changes necessary to attract private investors, but Mexico's divided government has been unwilling or unable to come to any agreement on new policies or legal changes.[35]

Access to natural gas and LPG distribution is also a problem in rural areas, but the causes are primarily related to the country's poor secondary and tertiary roads and are therefore not central to this discussion.

Security Vulnerabilities

A final but highly relevant area of discussion regarding Mexico's natural gas infrastructure is physical security. Critical infrastructure protection has long been a priority in the United States, and this has been even more the case since the 9-11 attacks. Unlike the United States, recent events have pointed not only to a reduced emphasis on infrastructure security in Mexico, but significant vulnerabilities as well. In 2007, a series of gas pipeline bombings were conducted by a largely defunct Marxist group, Ejercito Popular Revolucionario (EPR); "The blasts forced some 20,000 people to flee their homes, and the disruption in domestic oil and gas supplies (exports reportedly were not affected) caused numerous businesses to shut down or reduce their operations."[36] These attacks created alarm not only in Mexico but in the United States as well. That such a small and obscure group (presumably with limited resources) could cause such damage and disruption to Mexico's pipelines and gas distribution not only points to vulnerabilities in Mexico's infrastructure security, it may encourage other bad actors such as cartels or terrorist organizations to exploit these vulnerabilities for coercion and co-option in support of their own agendas. There are other indicators of inadequate infrastructure security as well, such as widespread illegal tapping of PEMEX pipelines, and security concerns have been raised in the international business community.[37] Mexico must work to properly address critical infrastructure protection in order to ensure future private investment and economic growth.

Conclusions and Recommendations

Mexico's natural gas transportation and distribution networks are plagued by inadequacy, in both quantity and quality, from well-head to burner-head. This situation, which threatens the nation's economic future, was caused by decades of indifference and neglect by PEMEX and the government towards development and sustainment of the natural gas industry. Many of the poor or shortsighted business practices by PEMEX were driven by fiscal constraints resulting from the government's heavy dependence on the company's revenues, but PEMEX has also been hampered in its ability to leverage private investment and ownership in developing and improving infrastructure due to legal and constitutional roadblocks and political infighting.[38] Despite these rather harsh realities regarding its natural gas infrastructure and the limited past success in addressing them, Mexico does have the potential, both in natural resources and options for private investment, to stimulate rapid and widespread infrastructure growth. Three options that offer the greatest likelihood of success are to open up natural gas production to private investment/involvement, increase and stabilize the annual funds available to PEMEX for reinvestment, and overhaul regulatory policies governing private and public-private contracting.

As discussed, private investment in oil or gas production in Mexico would require an amendment to the constitution, and past efforts along this path (most recently by President Calderon and other members of the PAN) have met with staunch resistance from the PRI and the PRD. However, opening up to private investment is a proven means of boosting production, with neighboring countries like Peru, Venezuela, Argentina and Brazil all doing so in the past decade or more. This is particularly noteworthy because these countries originally modeled their state-owned oil companies after Mexico's, but unlike Mexico they

15

have had the vision and leadership to make the necessary changes to remain competitive in the modern marketplace.[39] To break the current stalemate on this issue in Mexico, a tri-partisan effort of like-minded political leaders will be needed. It has been noted however, that such a concerted effort is unlikely, "[T]he mere mention of liberalizing these costly endeavors provokes the wrath of a PRI-PRD legislative bloc that has yet to offer a sound alternative plan."[40] One means of potentially countering the PRI-PRD bloc is to blunt the political capital they have traditionally gained, from fanning the nationalistic fervor, by informing and educating the public about the proven methods and benefits of allowing for and regulating private investment without jeopardizing the nation's resources.

Ensuring that PEMEX has adequate funds to re-invest in infrastructure each year seems obvious from a business perspective, but as discussed this has not occurred. With almost two thirds of its annual revenues going toward taxes (representing nearly roughly 40% of the federal budget), PEMEX has been essentially bled dry and lacks the funds and in-house ability to address all its woes.[41] While the accumulated damage from decades of undercapitalization cannot be undone overnight, taking the first step back should not be put off any longer. The Mexican government needs to work with the leadership within PEMEX to identify and establish annual funding for re-investment that is in line with commercial industry norms. While this will mean reduced government revenue from PEMEX in the short term, it promises to bring significant increases in overall revenue in the future, both from PEMEX and from the economic growth that a healthy natural gas operation will bring.

Regulatory reform is a third and critical area where Mexico must take action. Current policies for private investment prevent incentives and other inducements common in the rest of the world and also place an inordinate amount of risk on investors. The result has been a general lack of interest by the business community.[42] Likewise, many existing policies implemented over the years to prevent corruption have become so convoluted that it is difficult for PEMEX to make any progress even when complying with the existing frameworks for private contracts.[43] Another issue that should be resolved is the dichotomy between how PEMEX's gas operations are structured as compared to the rest of industry. PEMEX retains a monopoly on production and marketing of natural gas while trying to lure private investment and competition in transportation and distribution, but the natural gas business lends itself towards the opposite arrangement, with competitive production and marketing and monopolized transportation and distribution. By maintaining such policies and practices contrary to worldwide industry norms, PEMEX has caused many potential private investors to opt out.[44] This is especially apparent with the duration of exclusivity that PEMEX offers for gas distribution franchises; the standard for exclusivity ranges from 20 to 75 years or more in much of the world, but in Mexico it is a mere 12 years.[45] Given the large initial investment needed to construct gas transportation and distribution infrastructure, 12 years exclusivity does not offer investors much surety that the investment will be profitable and is a likely reason why many such contracts that have been put up for bid have had no takers. By implementing these legal and regulatory reforms to better incentivize contracts and lower risk, greatly increased private investment could be had by Mexico.

While a large portion of the solution lies with better support and management of PEMEX, to fund all or even a majority of the needed infrastructure expansion requires private investment. This can be done, and has been done elsewhere, in a manner that does not jeopardize sovereignty over national resources or proper oversight of industry. None of it will be possible however, unless the political in-fighting and obstructionism currently at play

amongst the PRI, PRD, and PAN can be set aside for the greater good of the country.

Endnotes

[1] Howard J. Wiarda and Harvey F. Kline, *Latin American Politics and Development* (Boulder: Westview Press, 2007): 395-396.

[2] Index Mundi, "Mexico GDP (purchasing power parity)," IndexMundi, accessed September 30, 2011, http://www.indexmundi.com/mexico/gdp_(purchasing_power_parity).html.

[3] Ewell E. Murphy Jr, "The prospect for further energy privatization in Mexico," *Texas International Law Journal* 36, no.1 (2001): 76, ProQuest (213922280).

[4] Braden Webb, "Demerits of Pemex Privatization," *Washington Report on the Hemisphere* 28, no.13 (2008):2, ProQuest (196338451).

[5] Ibid., 76

[6] Braden Webb, "Demerits of Pemex Privatization," 2.

[7] Ewell E. Murphy Jr, "The prospect for further energy privatization in Mexico," 76.

[8] Ibid., 5.

[9] The Economist, "The Americas: Running just to stand still," *The Economist* 385, no.8560 (2007): 77, ProQuest (223997977).

[10] Braden Webb, "Demerits of Pemex Privatization," 4.

[11] Michelle Michot Foss, "The Natural Gas Industry in Mexico: Markets vs. Government," *Revue de l'energie* 53, no.1 (2002):648.

[12] Juan Rosellon and Jonathan Halpern, "Regulatory Reform in Mexico's Natural Gas Industry: Liberalization in the Context of a Dominant Upstream Incumbent," The World Bank: Policy Research Working Paper 2537, January 2001, 13, http://www-wds.worldbank.org/external/default/main?pagePK=64187835&piPK=64620093&theSitePK=523679&lang=&sType=2&query=wps2537&cntry=&isLeftNav=N&pageSize=10&docType=0&sortOrderby=DOCDT&siteName=EXTWDS&menuPK=64187511&callBack=null&sortDesc=ORASCORE&dAtts=ORASCORE%2CDOCDT%2CDOCNA%2CDOCTY%2CSECCL%2CLANG%2CREPNB%2CVOLNB%2CREPNME%2CVOL_TITLE

[13] *Mexico Oil and Gas Report Q3 2011*, (London: Business Monitor International, 2011) http://www.businessmonitor.com/cgi-bin/request.pl?view=publicationsearch&productCode=SSMX02&service=2&pdfsearchtype=2&industryID=2&SessionID=A253399EFFF011E095A09A868A5BC7E4&target=Related%20Reports&iso=MX (accessed September 20, 2011), 43-44.

[14] Petroleos Mexicanos, "Methane to Markets: Mexico Oil and Natural Gas Country Profile," Global Methane, accessed on October 6th, 2011, http://www.globalmethane.org/documents/oilgas_cap_mexico.pdf

[15] Ibid., 38.

[16] Webb, "Demerits of Pemex Privatization," 2.

[17] "Ultraprofundas," El siglo de Torreon, March 24, 2008, quoted in Braden Webb, "Demerits of Pemex Privatization," *Washington Report on the Hemisphere* 28, no.13 (2008):2, ProQuest (196338451).

[18] Juan Rosellon and Jonathan Halpern, "Regulatory Reform in Mexico's Natural Gas Industry," 3.

[19] Raul Monteforte, "Gas-demand growth will push expansion in Mexican transmission infrastructure," Oil & Gas Journal 100, no.6 (2002):70-71, ProQuest (274426040).

[20] Cathy Suykens, "Gas Flaring in Developing Countries – Need for Kyoto Mechanisms or Sectoral Crediting Mechanisms?" Carbon & Climate Law Review 4, no.1 (2010):42, ProQuest (603212089).

[21] Business Monitor International, *Mexico Oil & Gas Report Q3 2011,* 32.

[22] "Production," PetroStrategies, Inc., last modified October 11, 2011, http://www.petrostrategies.org/Learning_Center/production.htm .

[23] "CO2 Injection Boosts Oil Recovery, Captures Emissions," Science Daily, January 10, 2005, http://www.sciencedaily.com/releases/2005/01/050110091718.htm .

[24] Juan Rosellon and Jonathan Halpern, "Regulatory Reform in Mexico's Natural Gas Industry," 5.

[25] Webb, "Demerits of Pemex Privatization," 2.

[26] "Industry Glossary," Sprague Energy, accessed October 6, 2011, http://www.spragueenergy.com/pages/content.aspx?p=Glossary

[27] Juan Rosellon and Jonathan Halpern, "Regulatory Reform in Mexico's Natural Gas Industry," 13, 28.

[28] Raul Monteforte, "Gas-demand growth will push expansion in Mexican transmission infrastructure," 71.

[29] Claudio F. Urencia and Juan Manuel Paz, "SCADA focus of Pemex gas pipeline network upgrade," Oil & Gas Journal 100, no.6 (2002): 76, ProQuest (274296548).

[30] Juan Rosellon and Jonathan Halpern, "Regulatory Reform in Mexico's Natural Gas Industry," 22, 28.

[31] Business Monitor International, *Mexico Oil & Gas Report Q3 2011,* 33, 43-45.

[32] Raul Monteforte, "Gas-demand growth will push expansion in Mexican transmission infrastructure," 74-75.

[33] Juan Rosellon and Jonathan Halpern, "Designing Natural Gas Distribution Concessions in a Megacity: Tradeoffs between Scale Economies and Information Disclosure in Mexico City," The World Bank: Policy Research Working Paper 2538, January 2004, 1, http://www-wds.worldbank.org/external/default/main?pagePK=64187835&piPK=64620093&theSitePK=523679&lang=&sType=2&query=wps2538&cntry=&isLeftNav=N&pageSize=10&docType=0&sortOrderby=DOCDT&siteName=EXTWDS&menuPK=64187511&callBack=null&sortDesc=ORASCORE&dAtts=ORASCORE%2CDOCDT%2CDOCNA%2CDOCTY%2CSECCL%2CLANG%2CREPNB%2CVOLNB%2CREPNME%2CVOL_TITLE

[34] Raul Monteforte, "Gas-demand growth will push expansion in Mexican transmission infrastructure," 75.

[35] The World Bank, *Private Solutions for Infrastructure in Mexico* (Washington, DC: The International Bank for Reconstruction and Development, 2003), 2-3, 36-37.

[36] The Economist, "Pipeline Bombs," September 13, 2007, ProQuest (208738881).

[37] Business Monitor International, *Mexico Oil & Gas Report Q3 2011,* 29, 60.

[38] Michelle Michot Foss, "The Natural Gas Industry in Mexico," 650.

[39] Ewell E. Murphy Jr, "The prospect for further energy privatization in Mexico," 76.

[40] Manuel Pastor and Carol Wise. "The Lost Sexenio: Vicente Fox and the New Politics of Economic Reform in Mexico." *Latin American Politics and Society* 47, no. 4 (2005): 147-150, ProQuest (200243308).

[41] "Blocked in Mexico," *Economist.Com / News Analysis,* May 7, 2008, ProQuest (208724656).

[42] The World Bank, *Private Solutions for Infrastructure in Mexico* (Washington, DC: The International Bank for Reconstruction and Development, 2003), 2-3.

[43] The Economist, "The Americas," 77.

[44] The World Bank, *Private Solutions for Infrastructure in Mexico* (Washington, DC: The International Bank for Reconstruction and Development, 2003), 3, 37.

[45] Juan Rosellon and Jonathan Halpern, "Regulatory Reform in Mexico's Natural Gas Industry," 16.

Bibliography

"The Americas: Running just to Stand Still; Mexico," *The Economist,* December 22, 2007, 77. ProQuest (223997977).

"Betting on Infrastructure Spending." *Country Monitor* 16, no. 37 (2008) 8. ProQuest (201755136).

Baker, George. Mexican Energy Sector Reforms Include Foreign Operators' Participation in E&D. *Oil & Gas Journal,* February 11, 2002. 64. ProQuest (274500923).

"Blocked in Mexico," *Economist.Com / News Analysis,* May 07, 2008. ProQuest (208724656).

"CO2 Injection Boosts Oil Recovery, Captures Emissions." *Science Daily*, January 10, 2005. http://www.sciencedaily.com/releases/2005/01/050110091718.htm

Deichmann, Uwe, Marianne Fay, Jun Koo, and Somik V. Lall. "Economic Structure, Productivity, and Infrastructure Quality in Southern Mexico." *The Annals of Regional Science* 38, no. 3 (2004) 361-385. ProQuest (194675329).

I-Chun, Chen. "Mexico'a Bottleneck to Fast Economic Growth." *Global Finance* 14, no. 10 (2000) 93-94. ProQuest (198843801).

Index Mundi, "Mexico GDP (purchasing power parity)." http://www.indexmundi.com/mexico/gdp_(purchasing_power_parity).html (accessed September 30, 2011).

Business Monitor International, *Mexico Oil and Gas Report Q3 2011*. London: Business Monitor International, 2011. http://www.businessmonitor.com/cgi-bin/request.pl?view=publicationsearch&productCode=SSMX02&service=2&pdfsearchtype=2&industryID=2&SessionID=A253399EFFF011E095A09A868A5BC7E4&target=Related%20Reports&iso=MX

Monteforte, Raul. "Gas-Demand Growth Will Push Expansion in Mexican Transmission Infrastructure," *Oil & Gas Journal,* Feb 11, 2002, 70. ProQuest (274426040).

Murphy, Ewell E., Jr. "The Prospect for further Energy Privatization in Mexico." *Texas International Law Journal* 36, no. 1 (2001) 75-97. ProQuest (213922280).

Ontiveros Padilla, Luis,E., "Mexican LPG Pipelines Juggle Product Mix with Variety of End Users," *Oil & Gas Journal,* Jun 24, 2002, 64. ProQuest (274279400).

Pappalardo, Joe. "U.S.-MEXICO Rapport Transformed by Terrorist Threat." *National Defense* 89, no. 609 (2004) 64-66. ProQuest (213365521).

Pastor, Manuel and Carol Wise. "The Lost Sexenio: Vicente Fox and the New Politics of Economic Reform in Mexico." *Latin American Politics and Society* 47, no. 4 (2005) 135-162. ProQuest (200243308).

Petroleos Mexicanos, "Methane to Markets: Mexico Oil and Natural Gas Country Profile," Global Methane. http://www.globalmethane.org/documents/oilgas_cap_mexico.pdf (accessed on October 6th, 2011).

PetroStrategies, Inc., "Production." http://www.petrostrategies.org/Learning_Center/production.htm (accessed October 14, 2011).

"Pipeline Bombs," *Economist.Com / News Analysis,* Sep 13, 2007, 1. ProQuest (208738881).

Rivas, Marcela Gonzalez. "Trade Openness, Infrastructure, and the Wellbeing of Mexico's South." *Mexican Studies* 27, no. 2 (2011) 407-429. ProQuest (883988229).

Rosellon, Juan and Jonathan Halpern, "Designing Natural Gas Distribution Concessions in a Megacity: Tradeoffs between Scale Economies and Information Disclosure in Mexico City," The World Bank: Policy Research Working Paper WPS2538, January 2004. http://www-wds.worldbank.org/external/default/main?pagePK=64187835&piPK=64620093&theSitePK=523679&lang=&sType=2&query=wps2538&cntry=&isLeftNav=N&pageSize=10&docType=0&sortOrderby=DOCDT&siteName=EXTWDS&menuPK=64187511&callBack=null&sortDesc=ORASCORE&dAtts=ORASCORE%2CDOCDT%2CDOCNA%2CDOCTY%2CSECCL%2CLANG%2CREPNB%2CVOLNB%2CREPNME%2CVOL_TITLE

Rosellon, Juan and Jonathan Halpern, "Regulatory Reform in Mexico's Natural Gas Industry: Liberalization in the Context of a Dominant Upstream Incumbent," The World Bank: Policy Research Working Paper WPS2537, January 2001. http://www-wds.worldbank.org/external/default/main?pagePK=64187835&piPK=64620093&theSitePK=523679&lang=&sType=2&query=wps2537&cntry=&isLeftNav=N&pageSize=10&docType=0&sortOrderby=DOCDT&siteName=EXTWDS&menuPK=64187511&callBack=null&sortDesc=ORASCORE&dAtts=ORASCORE%2CDOCDT%2CDOCNA%2CDOCTY%2CSECCL%2CLANG%2CREPNB%2CVOLNB%2CREPNME%2CVOL_TITLE

Sprague Energy, "Industry Glossary."
http://www.spragueenergy.com/pages/content.aspx?p=Glossary
(accessed October 6, 2011).

Suykens, Cathy. "Gas Flaring in Developing Countries - Need for Kyoto Mechanisms or
Sectoral Crediting Mechanisms?." *Carbon & Climate Law Review*. 4. no. 1 (2010)
42-50. ProQuest (603212089).

"Ultraprofundas." El siglo de Torreon. March 24, 2008. Quoted in Braden Webb, "Demerits
of Pemex Privatization," *Washington Report on the Hemisphere* 28, no.13 (2008):2,
ProQuest (196338451).

Urencio, Claudio F. and Juan Manuel Paz. SCADA Focus of Pemex Gas Pipeline Network
Upgrade. *Oil & Gas Journal,* Feb 11, 2002, 76-78. ProQuest (274296548).

Webb, Braden. *Demerits of Pemex Privatization*. United States, Washington: The Council on
Hemispheric Affairs, 2008. ProQuest (196638451).

Wiarda, Howard J., and Harvey F. Kline. *Latin American Politics and Development*.
Boulder, CO: Westview Press, 2007.

World Bank, *Private Solutions for Infrastructure in Mexico*. Washington, D.C.: The
International Bank for Reconstruction and Development, 2003.
http://www-wds.worldbank.org/external/default/main?pagePK=64193027&piPK=64187937&theSitePK=523679&menuPK=64187510&searchMenuPK=64187283&theSitePK=523679&entityID=000090341_20040818111500&searchMenuPK=64187283&theSitePK=523679
http://www.worldbank.org/reference/